WELCOMING WORDS

A Sesame Street Language Guide for Making Friends

J. P. Press

Lerner Publishing ◆ Minneapolis

Dear Parents and Educators,

From its very beginning, *Sesame Street* has promoted mutual respect and cultural understanding by featuring a cast of diverse and lovable characters. *Welcoming Words* introduces children to the wonderful, wide world we live in. In this book, *Sesame Street* friends present handy and fun vocabulary in six languages kids may not know. These words can help young readers welcome new friends. Have fun as you explore!

Sincerely,

The Editors at Sesame Workshop

Table of Contents

WELCOME TO
SPANISH

WELCOME!

¡Bienvenido!
(Say BYEN-veh-
NEE-doh)

How to Speak Spanish

Practice speaking Spanish! Each word is broken up into sounds called syllables. Do you see the syllable in CAPITAL LETTERS? That's the sound you emphasize the most!

Hello.

Hola.

OH-la

This is Abelardo.
He lives in Mexico.

What is your name?
¿Cómo te llamas?
KOH-moh teh YAH-mahs

My name is . . .
Me llamo . . .
meh YAH-moh . . .

friendship
amistad
ah-mees-tahd

Will you be my friend?
¿Quieres ser mi amigo?
KYEHR-ays sehr
mee ah-MEE-goh

Meet my family!

¡Conoce a mi familia!

koh-NOH-say ah mee
fah-MEE-lee-ah

dad
papá
pah-PAH

mom
mamá
mah-MAH

brother
hermano
ehr-MAH-noh

sister
hermana
ehr-MAH-nah

grandma
abuela
ah-BWAY-lah

grandpa
abuelo
ah-BWAY-loh

Thank you.
Gracias.
GRAH-see-ahs

You are welcome.
De nada.
deh NAH-dah

Please.
Por favor.
pore fah-VORE

I'm sorry.
Lo siento.
loh see-EHN-toh

lunch
almuerzo
ahl-MWEHR-soh

breakfast
desayuno
des-ah-YOO-noh

snack
refrigerio
reh-free-HEH-ree-oh

dinner
cena
SEH-nah

I'm thirsty.
Tengo sed.
TEHN-goh SED

I'm hungry.
Tengo hambre.
TEHN-goh HAHM-bray

Cookie Monster hungry.
Cookie Monster tiene hambre.

How are you?
¿Cómo estás?
KOH-moh ehs-TAHS

I'm fine, thank you.
Estoy bien, gracias.
ehs-TOY BYEHN GRAH-see-ahs

I like you.
Me agradas.
meh ah-GRAH-dahs

Elmo loves you.
Elmo te quiere.

happy
contento
cohn-TEN-toh

grumpy
malhumorado
mal-oo-more-ADOH

22

proud
orgulloso
or-goo-YOH-soh

excited
emocionado
eh-moh-see-oh-NAH-doh

dog
perro
PEH-roh

animals
animales
ah-nee-MAHL-ehs

fish
pez
PESS

bird
pájaro
PAH-ha-roh

cat
gato
GAH-toh

I like animals.

Me gustan los animales.

colors
colores
coh-LOH-rehs

My favorite color is . . .
Mi color favorito es . . .
mee cohl-OR
fah-vore-EE-toh
ess . . .

red
rojo
ROH-ho

orange
naranja
nah-RAHN-hah

yellow
amarillo
ah-mah-REE-yoh

green
verde
VEHR-deh

blue
azul
ah-ZOOL

purple
púrpura
POOR-poo-rah

Let's play!
¡Juguemos!
hoo-GAY-mohs

toys
juguetes
hoo-GEH-tehs

What do you like to do?
¿Qué te gusta hacer?
kay teh GOO-stah
ah-SEHR

We love to learn.

Nos encanta aprender.

Goodbye.
Adiós.
ah-DEEOS

See you soon!
¡Hasta pronto!
AH-stah PROHN-toh

Count It!

1 one
uno
OO-noh

2 two
dos
DOHS

3 three
tres
TREHS

4 four
cuatro
KWAH-tro

5 five
cinco
SEEN-koh

6 six
seis
SAYSS

7 seven
siete
see-EH-teh

8 eight
ocho
OH-cho

9 nine
nueve
noo-EH-veh

10 ten
diez
dee-ESS

Rosita's Favorite Words

I love music!
¡Me encanta
la música!

singing
cantar
cahn-TAHR

guitar
guitarra
ghee-TAH-rah

WELCOME TO
FRENCH

WELCOME!

Bienvenue!
(Say bee-ehn-ven-OOH)

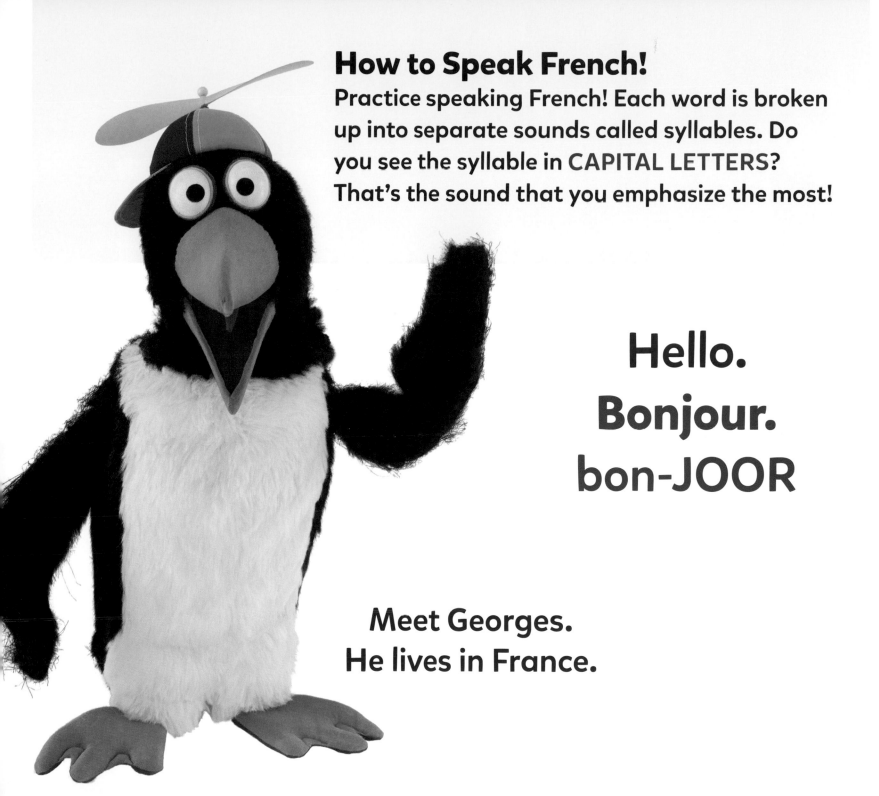

How to Speak French!

Practice speaking French! Each word is broken up into separate sounds called syllables. Do you see the syllable in CAPITAL LETTERS? That's the sound that you emphasize the most!

Hello.
Bonjour.
bon-JOOR

Meet Georges.
He lives in France.

What is your name?
Comment tu t'appelles?
koh-MOH too tah-pell

My name is . . .
Je m'appelle . . .
juh mah-PEHLL . . .

Will you be my friend?
Veux-tu être mon amie?
vuh TOO eh-tre mone
ah-MEE

friendship
amitié
ah-mee-tee-AY

best
friends

meilleurs
amis

may-URS
ah-MEE

This is my family!
Voilà, c'est ma famille!

42

dad
papa
pah-PA

mom
maman
mah-MA

brother
frère
frair

sister
sœur
seure

grandma
grand-mère
grahn-MAIR

grandpa
grand-père
grahn-PAIR

Thank you.
Merci.
mair-SEE

You are welcome.
De rien.
duh ree-AIN

Please.
S'il vous plaît.
seel voo PLAY

I'm sorry.
Je suis désolé.
juh SWEE
day-so-LAY

45

breakfast
petit déjeuner
puh-TEE day-
juh-NAY

lunch
déjeuner
day-juh-NAY

dinner
dîner
dee-NAY

hungry
affamé
ah-fah-MAY

thirsty
assoiffé
ah-swa-FAY

Cookie Monster wants a snack.

Cookie Monster veut une collation.

How are you?
Comment allez-vous?
koh-MOH tal-AY-voo

I'm fine, thank you.
Bien, merci.
bee-EHN mair-SEE

**This is Griotte.
She's from France.**

I like you.
Je t'aime.
juh TEM

happy
heureux
heu-REU

grumpy
grincheux
grain-SHEU

proud
fier
fee-AIR

excited
enthousiaste
ehn-thoo-see-AH-ste

51

dog
chien
SHE-eh

fish
poisson
pwa-SOH

bird
oiseau
wah-ZO

cat
chat
sha

animals
animaux
ah-nee-MO

colors
couleurs
coo-LEHR

My favorite
color is . . .
Ma couleur
préférée est . . .
mah coo-LEHR
pray-fay-RAY
ay . . .

red
rouge
roo-je

orange
orange
oh-rhan-JE

yellow
jaune
JHO-ne

green
vert
vair

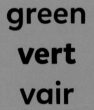

blue
bleu
bluh

purple
violet
vee-oh-LAY

55

Let's play!
On va jouer!
ohn vah joo-AY

toys
jouets
joo-AY

Goodbye.
Au revoir.
oh re-VWAR

See you soon!
À bientôt !
AH bee-ehn-TOE

59

Count It!

1 one
un
uhn

2 two
deux
deuh

3 three
trois
twah

4
four
quatre
CAT-re

7
seven
sept
set

5
five
cinq
sank

8
eight
huit
weet

6
six
six
seeseh

9
nine
neuf
nuhf

10
ten
dix
deese

magic
magique
mah-JICK

magic wand
baguette magique
bah-GET mah-JICK

fairy
fée
faye

WELCOME TO GERMAN

WELCOME!

Herzlich willkommen!

HERTZ-lih VEEL-koh-men

How to Speak German!

Practice speaking German! Each word is broken up into separate sounds called syllables. Do you see the syllable in CAPITAL LETTERS? That's the sound that you emphasize the most!

Some words in German change a little for men and women. In this book we switch back and forth.

Hello.
Hallo.
HA-lo

This is Finchen.
He lives in Germany.

My name is . . .
Ich heiße . . .
eeh HEIS-uh . . .

67

friendship
freundschaft
FROIND-shahft

friend
freund
froind

**Will you be
my friend?**
**Willst du meine
Freundin sein?**
villst doo MY-nuh
FROIN-deen sine

Meet my family!
Lerne meine Familie kennen!
LAIR-nuh MY-nuh FAH-mih-lee KE-nen

dad
papa
PA-pa

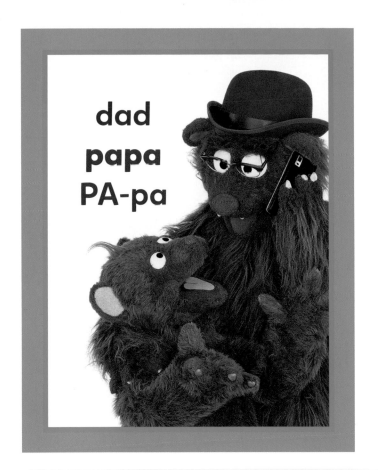

mom
mama
MA-ma

brother
bruder
BROO-der

sister
schwester
SHVES-ter

grandma
oma
OH-ma

grandpa
opa
OH-pa

Thank you.
Danke.

You are welcome.
Bitte schön.
BIT-uh shoon

**Please.
Bitte.
BIT-uh**

**I'm sorry.
Es tut mir leid.
es toot meer lide**

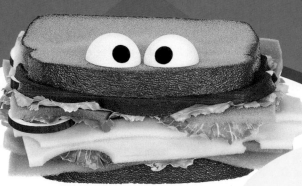

**lunch
mittagessen
mih-tag-ESS-en**

**breakfast
frühstück
FROO-schtuhk**

**snack
snack
snehck**

**dinner
abendessen
ahb-end-ESS-en**

I'm thirsty. hungry
Ich bin durstig. **hungrig**
eeh bin DUHR-schtick HUN-grick

How are you?
Wie geht es dir?
vee get es dihr

I'm fine, thank you.
Mir geht es gut, danke.
meer get es guht, DAWN-kuh

I like you.
Ich mag dich.
eeh mag dih

happy
glücklich
GLOOK-lih

sad
traurig
TROW-rig

proud
stolz
schtohltz

excited
aufgeregt
OWF-geh-rehgt

dog
hund
hoondt

animals
tiere
TIER-uh

fish
fisch
fish

cat
katze
KAT-zuh

hamster
hamster
HAHM-stair

I like animals.

Ich mag Tiere.

colors
farben
FAHR-ben

My favorite color is . . .
Meine Lieblingsfarbe ist . . .
MY-nuh LEEB-lings-FAHR-buh ist . . .

red
rot
roht

orange
orange
OH-rawnge

yellow
gelb
gelb

green
grün
groon

blue
blau
blauw

purple
lila
LEE-la

Let's play!
Lass uns spielen!
lahs oonz
SCHPEEL-en

toys
spielsachen
SCHPEEL-saw-hen

What do you like to do?
Was möchtest du gerne tun?
vahs MOH-test doo
GAIR-nuh toon

Goodbye.
Auf Wiedersehen.
owf VEE-der-sane

See you soon!
Bis bald!

Count It!

1 one **eins** eintz

2 two **zwei** svy

3 three **drei** dry

4 four
vier
fear

5 five
fünf
foonf

6 six
sechs
zex

7 seven
sieben
ZEE-ben

8 eight
acht
awkt

9 nine
neun
noin

10 ten
zehn
tzen

Bert and Ernie's Favorite Words

bubbles
schaum
shaum

bird
vogel
FOH-gull

stripes
streifen
SHTRIE-fen

It's bath time! Zeit zum Baden!

WELCOME TO HEBREW

WELCOME!

בָּרוּךְ הַבָּא!

(Say ba-RUKH ha-BA)

How to Speak Hebrew

Did you know that the Hebrew alphabet uses different letters? You read it from right to left. Practice speaking Hebrew! Each word is broken up into separate sounds called syllables. Do you see the syllable in CAPITAL LETTERS? That's the sound that you emphasize the most!

Hello.

שָׁלוֹם.

sha-LOM

This is Avigail.
She lives in Israel.

What is your name?

אֵיךְ קוֹרְאִים לָךְ?

EYKH kor-IM lach?

My name is . . .

קוֹרְאִים לִי . . .

kor-IM LI . . .

95

friendship
חֲבֵרוּת
kha-ve-RUT

best friends
חֲבֵרִים הֲכִי טוֹבִים
kha-ve-REEM
ha-KHI to-VEEM

Will you be my friend?

רוֹצֶה לִהְיוֹת חָבֵר שֶׁלִּי?

ro-TZE li-HYOT
kha-VER she-LI

Meet
my family!

הַכֵּר אֶת
מִשְׁפַּחְתִּי!

dad

אַבָּא

A-ba

mom

אִמָּא

EE-ma

brother

אָח

AKH

sister

אָחוֹת

a-KHOT

grandma

סַבְתָא

SAV-ta

grandpa

סַבָּא

SA-ba

Thank you.
תּוֹדָה.
toe-DA

Please.

בְּבַקָשָׁה.

be-va-ka-SHA

I'm sorry.

אֲנִי מִצְטַעֵר.

a-NI mitz-ta-ER

breakfast
אֲרוּחַת בּוֹקֶר
a-ru-KHAT
BO-ker

lunch
אֲרוּחַת צָהֳרַיִים
a-ru-KHAT
tzo-ha-RA-im

dinner
אֲרוּחַת עֶרֶב
a-ru-KHAT
eh-rev

thirsty

צָמֵא

tza-MEH

This is Moishe Oofnik. He is from Israel.

103

How are you?

מָה שְׁלוֹמְךָ?

MA shlom-KHA

**This is Brosh.
He lives in
Israel.**

I'm fine, thank you.

אֲנִי בְּסֵדֶר תּוֹדָה.

a-NI be-SE-der to-DA

I like you.

אֲנִי מְחַבֵּב אוֹתְךָ.

a-NI me-kha-BEV
ot-KHA

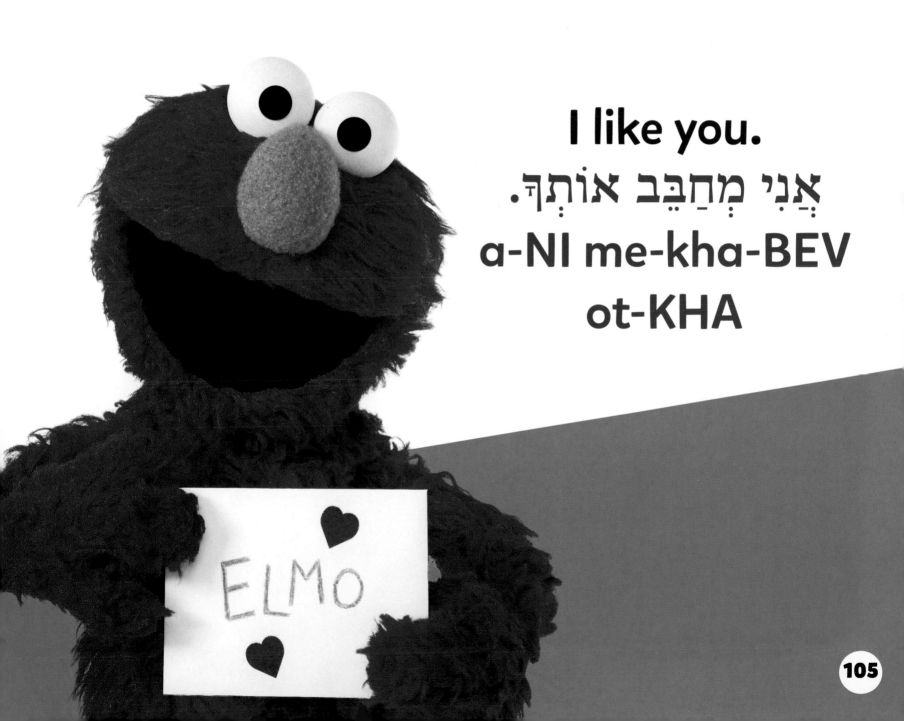

happy
שָׂמֵחַ
sa-MEH-akh

I feel grumpy.
אֲנִי מַרְגִּיש עַצְבָּנִי.

106

proud
גֵּאֶה

geh-EH

excited
נִרְגָּשׁ

nir-GASH

dog
כֶּלֶב
KEH-lev

animals
חַיּוֹת
kha-YOT

fish
דָּג
DAG

bird
צִיפּוֹר
tzi-POR

cat
חָתוּל
kha-TUL

Let's look at colors!

בּוֹא נִסְתַּכֵּל עַל צְבָעִים!

My favorite color is . . .

. . . הַצֶּבַע הָאָהוּב עָלַי הוּא

ha-TZE-va ha-a-HUV

a-LAI HU . . .

red
אָדֹם
a-DOM

orange
כָּתֹם
ka-TOM

yellow
צָהֹוב
tza-HOV

green
יָרֹוק
ya-ROK

blue
כָּחֹול
ka-KHOL

purple
סָגֹל
sa-GOL

What do you like to do?
מָה אַתָּה אוֹהֵב לַעֲשׂוֹת?
MA a-TA o-HEV
la-a-SOT

toys
צַעֲצוּעִים
tza-a-tzu-IM

jump
לִקְפּוֹץ
lik-POTZ

Let's play!
בּוֹא נְשַׂחֵק!

**Meet Sivan.
She lives in Israel.**

Goodbye.

לְהִתְרָאוֹת.

le-hit-ra-OT

See you soon!

נִתְרָאֶה בְּקָרוֹב!

nit-ra-EH be-ka-ROV

Count It!

1 one
אַחַת
a-KHAT

2 two
שְׁתַּיִם
SHTA-im

3 three
שָׁלוֹשׁ
sha-LOSH

4 four
אַרְבַּע
AR-ba

5 five
חָמֵשׁ
kha-MESH

6 six
שֵׁשׁ
SHESH

7 seven
שֶׁבַע
SHEH-va

8 eight
שְׁמוֹנֶה
SHMO-ne

9 nine
תֵּשַׁע
TE-sha

10 ten
עֶשֶׂר
EH-ser

Cookie Monster's Favorite Words

Are you hungry?
אַתָּה רָעֵב?

Yummy!
טָעִים!
ta-IM

snack
חֲטִיף
kha-TIF

cookies
עוּגִיוֹת
u-gi-YOT

WELCOME TO **ARABIC**

WELCOME!

أهلاً بك!

Say ah-LAAN-bika

120

How to Speak Arabic

Did you know that the Arabic alphabet uses different letters? You read it from right to left. Practice speaking Arabic! Each word is broken up into separate sounds called syllables. Do you see the syllable in CAPITAL LETTERS? That's the sound that you emphasize the most!

Hello.

مرحباً.

mar-HAB-aan

Meet No'man! He is from the United Arab Emirates (UAE).

What is your name?

ما اسمك؟

M-ism-UK

My name is . . .

اسمي . . .

is-MI . . .

friendship

صداقة

sa-DA-qa

Will you be my friend?

هل ستصبح صديقي؟

HAL-sa-TU-sbih-sa-dIqi

We are best friends!

نحن أفضل أصدقاء!

125

dad
أب
AB

mom
أم
UM

brother
أخ
AKH

sister
أخت
UKHT

grandma
جدة
JA-da

grandpa
جد
JAD

Thank you.

شكراً لك.

shkr-AAN-LA-ka

You are welcome.

عفواً.

af-WAN

Please.

رجاءً.

RA-ja

I'm sorry.

أنا آسف.

ANA-a-sif

breakfast
فطور
fvu-TOR

lunch
غداء
GHA-daa

dinner
عشاء
ash-aa

I'm thirsty.

أنا عطشان.

ana-at-SHAN

I'm hungry.

أنا جائع.

ANA-JA-yie

How are you?

كيف حالك؟

KAYF-HA-luk

I'm fine, thank you.

بخير، شكراً لك.

bi-KHAYR, shuk-RAAN-LA-ka

Meet Shams! She is from the UAE.

happy

مسرور

mas-RUR

sad

حزين

ha-ZIN

134

proud

فخور

FA-khur

excited

مبتهج

mub-TA-hij

animals
حيوانات
hay-WA-nat

fish
سمكة
sa-MA-ka

bird
عصفور
es-FOR

cat
قطة
qi-TA

My favorite color is . . .

لوني المفضل . . .

LA-wni-al-MU-fadal . . .

colors

ألوان

al-WAN

red

أحمر

ah-MAR

orange

برتقالي

burto-QA-li

yellow

أصفر

as-FAR

green

أخضر

akh-DAR

blue

أزرق

az-RAQ

purple

بنفسجي

ba-NA-fsaji

toys
ألعاب
al-AAB

jump
يقفز
YA-qfiz

What do you like to do?

ماذا تحب أن تعمل؟

MA-dha-tuhi-BU-AN-te-MAL

We like to play!

نحب أن نلعب!

Goodbye.

وداعاً.

wa-DA-an

See you soon!

أراك قريباً!

ar-AAK-qary-BAAN

Count It!

1 one
واحد
WA-hid

2 two
اثنان
eth-NAN

3 three
ثلاثة
tha-LA-tha

4 four
أربعة
ar-BA-a

5 five
خمسة
kham-SA

6 six
ستة
si-TA

7 seven
سبعة
sab-AA

8 eight
ثمانية
tha-MA-nia

9 nine
تسعة
tis-AA

10 ten
عشرة
ash-aa-RA

Elmo's Favorite Words

That tickles!

ذلك يضحك!

tha-li-KA-YU-dhik

Welcome to my home.

أهلاً بك في منزلي.

ahl-AAN-bi-KA-FI-MA-nzi-li

**Elmo is happy
to see you!**

Elmo مسرور برؤيتك!

El-MO-masr-UR-biru-a-YA-tik

WELCOME TO MANDARIN CHINESE

WELCOME!

欢迎!
(Say huān yíng)

How to Speak Mandarin Chinese

Mandarin Chinese can be written in a special system called Pinyin. Most letters in Pinyin sound the same as if you were reading English, but a few of the letters have slightly different sounds. For example, if you see a *c*, make the *ts* sound. This is how you would say the English sounds in Pinyin:

c = ts   x = sh   e = uh   ui =way
q = ch   z = dz   u = oo   i =ee

This is Lily. She lives in China.

Hello.
你好.
nǐ hǎo

Pinyin also shows you what tones to use with special accents on letters:

ē = flat tone, a little higher than regular speech
é = rising tone (like when you ask a question)
ě = falling, then rising tone
è = falling tone

What is your name?

你叫什么名字?

nǐ jiào shén me míng zi

My name is . . .

我叫...

wǒ jiào . . .

friendship
友谊
yǒu yì

Will you be my friend?
你愿意做我的朋友吗?
nǐ yuàn yì zuò wǒ de péng you ma

You're my best friend!

你是我最好的朋友！

family
家庭
jiā tíng

dad
爸爸
bà ba

This is
my mom.
这是我的妈妈.

brother
兄弟
xiōng di

sister
姐妹
jiě mèi

grandma
奶奶
nǎi nai

grandpa
爷爷
yé ye

Thank you.
谢谢.
xiè xie

You are welcome.
不客气.
bú kè qi

Please.
请.
qǐng

I'm sorry.
对不起.
duì bù qǐ

lunch
午餐
wǔ cān

breakfast
早餐
zǎo cān

snack
零食
líng shí

dinner
晚餐
wǎn cān

I'm thirsty.

我渴了.

wǒ kě le

How are you?

你好吗？
nǐ hǎo ma

I'm fine, thank you.

我很好，谢谢你.
wǒ hěn hǎo xiè xiè nǐ

I like you.
我喜欢你.
wǒ xǐ huan nǐ

happy
高兴
gāo xìng

sad
难过
nán guò

proud
骄傲
jiāo ào

excited
激动
jī dòng

163

dog
狗
gŏu

animals
动物
dòng wù

fish
鱼
yú

bird
鸟
niăo

cat
猫
māo

Animals
are great!
动物们真是
太有趣了！

colors
颜色
yán sè

My favorite color is . . .
页我最喜欢的颜色是 . . .
wǒ zuì xǐ huan de
yán sè shì . . .

red
红色
hóng sè

orange
橙色
chéng sè

yellow
黄色
huáng sè

green
绿色
lǜ sè

blue
蓝色
lán sè

purple
紫色
zǐ sè

167

Let's play!
我们一起玩吧!
wǒ men yì qǐ wán ba

toys
玩具
wán jù

What do you like to do?
你喜欢做什么?
nǐ xǐ huan zuò shén me

I like to jump.
我喜欢跳来跳去.

Goodbye.
再见
zài jiàn

See you soon!
回头见！
huí tóu jiàn

Count It!

1 one
— yī

2 two
二 èr

3 three
三 sān

4 four
四
sì

5 five
五
wǔ

6 six
六
liù

7 seven
七
qī

8 eight
八
bā

9 nine
九
jiǔ

10 ten
十
shí

Oscar's Favorite Words

I love trash!
我爱垃圾!

messy
乱糟糟的
luàn zāo zāo de

trash can
垃圾桶
lā jī tǒng

grumpy
暴躁的
bào zào de